STOPPING THE LIGHTS IN RANELAGH

Also by Macdara Woods:

Poetry:
"Decimal D. Sec. drinks in a Bar in Marrakesh", *New Writers' Press*, 1970.
"Early Morning Matins", *Gallery Press*, 1972.

Translation:
"The King of the Dead and Other Libyan Tales" (with the author Redwan Abushwesha), *Martin Brian & O'Keefe*, 1978.

Stopping The Lights In Ranelagh

MACDARA WOODS

DEDALUS

The Dedalus Press
46 Seabury, Sydney Parade Avenue, Sandymount, Dublin 4

© Macdara Woods 1987. Reprinted 1989.

All rights reserved.

ISBN 0 948268 25 5 (paper)

ACKNOWLEDGEMENTS: to
Aquarius (London), *Broadsheet, The Bunbrosna Stream, Cork Examiner, Cyphers, Drehpunkt* (Switzerland), *Irish Times, Lace Curtain, Poetry Ireland Review, Reality, Structure, The Cultural Weekly,* Tripoli (Libya), *Two Rivers,* (London).

Acknowledgement is also made to the Lamont Poetry Library at Harvard University.

The Dedalus Press acknowledges the assistance of An Chomhairle Ealaíon (The Arts Council) in the publication of this book.

Typesetting & make-up: Vermilion
Cover Design: Brendan Foreman

Contents

Cauchemar Is A White Horse................................7
The Drunken Ladies..8
And Until This Then So....................................9
Four Precepts..10
Credentials As It Were...................................11
The Sixteenth Kind Of Fear...............................12
First Letter For J.S.....................................13
Controlled and Intermittent Falling......................14
Cyphers 1 - 5..15
The Burning Tree In The Public Gardens...................18
Decimal's Liberal Schooling And After....................19
A Sea Of Rooves And Leaded Gables........................20
Release Papers...22
Falling Down Borges' Stairs..............................23
For Jack Walsh d. London 1973............................24
Derryribeen Westport, June 16th 1975.....................25
Leather Tourniquet.......................................26
Vade Mecum...27
Days of 1979 Morocco, Ten Years After....................28
Jack Walsh...29
Sequence For Carrington..................................30
For My Grandmother, Nora Wooloughan......................32
Cassandra Speaks About The Irish Famine..................34
The Wicked Messenger.....................................35
Knocking Holes In Fontainebleau..........................36
Ophelia, Sing To Me......................................38
O Bakelite Miz Moon......................................39
The Last Machine...41
Eight Hours To Prove The Artefact........................43
The Hospital Cafeteria...................................44
Shades Of Ranelagh.......................................45
Houserules...46
Three Figures In A Pub With Music........................47
Days Of May 1985...48
Closeup..49
Lazarus In Fade Street...................................51
Stopping The Lights, Ranelagh 1986.......................54

Epigraphs

Prohibido Prohibir
(Anarchist slogan on a wall in Barcelona)

A wondrous thing happened at sea: the water turned to bone.
(Riddle 69, Ice, The Exeter Book.)

Cauchemar Is A White Horse

Wear your hair like a skull cap
burning your brain; lay shoulders bare
like horses to hunger and thirst upon my energy,
for death and disease the offered groin.
One thousand years of horses' hooves
are beating here between twin stars
my eyes: come Cauchemar and ride our nights,
sweat yellow, sweet in the light lifting
from the eyes of Christ crossed in wire
staring in an ivy wind. Come Christ and Cauchemar,
my sweet mares till morning.

The Drunken Ladies

There was one drunken lady in Dublin
who ginned to sleep and cried
tell me love if we wake in the morning
but the boat had gone, the passage paid,
somebody slipped on the Dublin line.
There were five drunken ladies in Bayswater
the first was a red man's red haired daughter
or maybe his wife it was no great matter
when four were drunk then one was sober,
there were three drunken ladies in Fulham
who had gone when he went back to London again,
there were two drunken ladies in Paris but
no time to stop to ask their names
for the train was leaving the station and
there was one drunken lady in Spain.

And Until This Then So

   1.
And until this then so
   you sat all in all
beneath a willow tree; cool
where the leaves hung over your hair
and the branches held your face.
   And I, had I been there
would have held your face
between my hands, or with
my eyes perhaps.
   For, yes had I been there
I would await your smile, your
gesture of approval; and then
as sunlight underneath the willow tree
I would make known my will to you.

   2.
You see these lilies?
I have plucked them for the altar rails,
Unto the rough white lace once
I went, and leaned my chin upon
The cold of marble. Now I bring
These lilies, green and false as gas.

   3.
If you have not seen green and silver lights
On city trees, or morning over buildings
Under demon leaves then I would show you
Sleepless streets at dawn and no fantastic
Dawning this; but dawn, cold dawning
Seen in windows,
And your face grown cold and grey.

Four Precepts

1.
My woman wild in warmth has died
Alone in the cold sea towns
When the sea scattered her limbs wide

Late and naked she found
The lost shore of her body's pride.

2.
He who would be saint must dare
First the withering of youth,
And wandering strip love bare
To the teeth of his heart's truth.

3.
Mad woman to the young,
When she spoke with a wry mouth
Her words were strong

But when she turned south
From her heart's town,
Truth poisoned her tongue.

4.
When the raven first courts love
My love shall die to the black north bird,
Four cold seasons in the heart
Have taught me the sense of her words;

Four cold seasons in the heart broke earth
And the flame of the frost
Burned in her soul till her body scorched
In the dead fields of her youth's dust.

Credentials, As It Were

Five weeks upon the mountainside
crying in the solar wind —
something occurs in November —
it's poetry today and my feet are on fire
on fire my love again:
punctuating the mackerel roads. The
stroboscopic eyes of cars, the stares
no longer graze — a standard exercise
and I no longer fear the cold eyes.
The drowned water gives off air
for islands floating down the tide,
the limit of endurance is not to be afraid —
but to move onward as the gulls ride.
Then should I follow the horseriding clouds
to the unicorn well where morning breaks?
Following down the curlew paths
to where the lost wind waits. O state
a destination Countess: call the stakes
upon the green baize table-land,
the cards are turning in the railed box
and I don't hold the joker in the pack
though maybe healing fingers might unlock
the sunlight at the mind's back
and teach me how to laugh and play the deck.

The Sixteenth Kind Of Fear

Who was it moving the curtain then?
Only the wind; the hand of the wind.

And who was it making light dance in the wind?
Only the sea-light caressing the sun.

Who was that walking when night came down?
Just a night-watchman thinking of home.

And whose was the face at my mountain window?
Only a dead tree white as a bone.

Whose was the fever then, cold in the sun?
Only my love's when my love lies alone.

And who is the stranger I meet in the evening?
Only the future, love, coming and going.

First Letter For J.S.

Now if I had been wise then maybe I would make
A marble bell for you to toll the world

Across this doubting dog-watch lake of words. But
Sceptical as ever was — derisively unsure and frail

I am not wise and never was but something does remain
For I do hold some circuits in the mind, a wind

Whereby I can believe in different kinds of pain.
Listen though, geraniums bloomed in Lavender Gardens

When all your leaping words were said; eternally
Within that loss of sound your sorrow sharpened

All remembrance of the less than dead. The heads
Upon the balcony, the dipping heads of swans combined

With Leda and with lovers and with memory and mime.
But then I had no answer and so surely was not wise.

Come dance with me — you said — or could you dance
Or could you, dancing with me, redeem time? But

You knew I could not step into your anguished eyes
Without some fitting song or symbol to explain

Why I have such dependance upon such ruin of rhyme.
Could I reduce complexity and tell it to you plain.

Controlled And Intermittent Falling

I'm sailing my hoist 15 stories up
watching the truth through a chink in the boards
a piece of dislodged concrete turning slowly
like a lazy killer fish in water sinking down
the levels of floors
And if you were to ask I'd say
my circles of experience spiral in
like a zoomshot on a staircase —
dizzy to look up and dangerous to look down.
What wind will form me patterns now,
eccentric circles, fragments of stone?
perhaps the dancers and the strangers
who refuse to get it straight
the legend on my doorway reads
London: Cul de Sac.
turning the wheel by opposites they sharpened steel
for a punctured lung on a railway bridge,
an eye gouged out and sepsis from a dirty knife;
the houses shrinking on a razor's acid edge,
arterial roads, two rooms, a telly set;
Thursday noon, pay packets and perhaps a bet,
Guinness and Bitter — the leering Black and Tan —
offense, surprise if you object;
thing is that we were doing our best
to keep a troubled ship together
on bad sea roads where each port seemed
less likely than another.
A tree in Green Park must make do for a forest
a pool set in mortar make do for an ocean
a street full of windows must make do for sand dunes,
the one action open is captive; is walking
without speaking, without stopping, without turning.
and so, from fifteen stories up
some lives become apparent. A definition:
controlled and intermittent falling.

Cyphers One To Five

Cypher 1
   1.
Still, make no loving for any black town
Neither in the word's twin nor stranger's spit
And sound out no notions for a tired turn
Nor sell a single vision for a vision's worth.

   2.
And, since in no time such time swims past
Our self conceived deceived advice cuts fine
I know. Perhaps one woman told me right
She said — Respect the origins of line.

Cypher 2
   1.
I can fly, cried the mad castellan,
See, I can fly like a bat.
And at dawn and dusk he made radar sounds
Flapping his clerical cloth.
I can swim like a fish through the bars
Of St. Peter's tiered tiara;
And then in the evening livid with stars
I hang in the college of cardinals.

   2.
See, I can see, said the poet from prison
As he drew his teeth in the cellar.
So saying he considered the sun as a vision
And quietly cried out on angelic disorder.

Cypher 3
Ice, oh let him have ice for this is fire
This place-name elegy within the mind.

First hand he cries out on the highest power
Taking shelter in the castles of the Rhine.

Disorder me angels, disordered he cries
Pinned on the graph of Jacob and the Twins;

He has a blood red flower behind his eyes
That whispers outwards through his brain.

Cypher 4
  1.
The poet is dancing again friend Goethe
Tonight with his white haired girl
Norse lady of the horseman and the dying child.
He is riding and crying his visions to death
But too late again and always too late
For turret and tree top have crumbled to bone.

  2.
The moon is dancing tonight friend Goethe
Cold in the feathers of the sailing gulls.
Norse lady of the horseman and the dying child
In the jaw-bone night she bares her teeth
And wakes athirst for her liege lord hurled
Through his thousand years of gipsy sleep.

  3.
Scarlet and black is the step friend Goethe
Dancing with her murdered lord
Norse lady of the horseman and the dying child
She bleeds her visions and weights her words.
Yes; but something remains from every change
Though she splits refractions and poisons worlds.

Cypher 5
It is spring rain here but time remains
tuned cold. Gothic cloth in the stone
And Elijah the moonlight admiral drowns
In the sliding years for none catch hold.

Spring tide; neap tide; seasons lead on
For this one sailor who saw most clear
As when Elijah, the fabulous charioteer
He drove witch haired down see saw roads
Declaiming through eyes of water glass
His three card summer time pleasure boats
The cordage learned and the master rigged
To keep his ship-of-line loves afloat.

Deliver him this much Norse lady now
A white chart for return; how might he go and how
Re-engage with his terrible moons of war
For he fears their sharp and riding shapes,
In the pumpkin world their lanthorn teeth
Are spilling his dreams from mouth to mouth,
Who moves forever through an agony of wakes
To beach, a tendril mandrake of the rocks.

It is spring rain, yes, but time remains
And Elijah turned in the stone.

The Burning Tree In The Public Gardens

The burning tree in the public gardens
is not for surveying the swaying of curtains,
blue smoke whorling in the wind;
but the flame of that tree in a half-lit bedroom
could never scatter sunlight or shade. No tree remains,
but the image on the retina is scratched and stained.
Destruction of a childhood picture is mainly
reduction of spaces; the deck-chair in the public park
is an ass and cart on a Georgian roof. The ambuscade
of Tiger Lil and Tiger Moth, the Great Tall Ships,
the cards, the 'planes of the First World War,
are all gone to ground with my Grandfather's hand
that led me by times up Pembroke Street.
I remember too the whistling of trains when
I fell through the struts of a wet veranda onto the rails
and I called in a child's voice 'Granda, I'm safe
with the green balloons that float out with seagulls'
and pigeons sang in a church on the corner
and paid no tax on their black-framed windows but
coiled like lovers about the cross-struts
till their throats were silenced by builder's lime.
And now, perhaps because the tree is aflame,
the thought is constriction in the chest,
grey ash on a poised cigarette erect at an angle
between concrete fingers, belabouring what might have been
the good; in a tumbling of fiery wood the sparks
are red and leather phantoms in the dark.
The gombeen and goad are tearing down my childhood
— not brick by brick, but roof by stack
and leave me watching, at the age of thirty,
in the perfect teeth of these buildings a graveyard gap.

Decimal's Liberal Schooling — And After

Humanic, in deed, his mentors were
when first our Decimal drew breath
upon the flies that circled on his sight
and he learned to speak in chords;
Humanic, in deed, and dressed in black
(the evening star presages night
and Decimal is frightened of the dark
his birth-card is the ace of spades)
and so; Basilisk, remote, mosaic,
in the columned city of Volubilis
Alexander Helios and Cleopatra Silene
most ancient sun and moon as twins smile back
and the dark ace winks up gently from the pack
though touched and greased with finger marks
still such as opened many feasts. A stranger
hear the heart and two red kings at the door
crab claws scuttle and clutch and
Decimal runs through the streets in fear
for though in fact he's well informed
he reaches out an empty hand . . . and so

Black gentlemen in wings of black, he cries,
now give me something more than dust or chalk.

A Sea Of Rooves And Leaded Gables

A sea of rooves and leaded gables
made me feel easy in Paris
each in its way infamous as Casanova's
and each as much battened down; cone
upon cone in the morning, segmented,
opening on racy lines of washing;
on lives (Garlic and Gauloises climbing the air shaft
clearly misnomered a courtyard)
and the triangular shapes recede
becoming a morning-fluffed pigeon
or a blue boy whistling his way to decision —
the Lycée and rancour of leather.
The wine was good and the bread still better
though both remained from the night before;
hot coffee, cheese and apples on the parapet,
we hung like a bell in the frame of the building,
imaginary wings averted vertigo
and the curtains swung like a metronome.
In the night we flecked our eyes with sequins
and watched the yellow drops cascade
of Pernod poured in candle-light
and laughed and made love unafraid.
Waxlight wanes to morning; shapes remain
a brown ankle caught like a bird in the coverlet
an arm crooked lazily amain
two tangled bodies: les jeunes gens
en numero dix, Hôtel du Commerce
Rue de la Montagne Ste. Geneviève
and poems on the tiles like stains.
Trigonometry of course has rolled the bones —
would I at a distance know you again?

Not in mimosas, nor pine trees, nor bamboo,
not in the forests of the Ardennes
not in the geranium road to Alicante
not in the cornfield near Boulogne
not in the Berkshire haystacks we slept in
not by Dover Beach nor any ship's pitching.
In one place only perhaps I might find you
among walls and scree on the western seaboard
in the spray half blinded atop Dun Aengus
if your lips were salt and your smile were anxious
as under the willow you once smiled approval:
for it was not just time, love, that drove in the wedge.

Release Papers

Late October and I'm out
on a fair day you might say for Dublin
but a cold day for the breeze block Quasbah
down at the bottom of the garden. Its
lizard eyes thin slits of light
for the sun to hide in corners.
Kennedy's snug is shaped like a ship
time and the clock collide
forever taking each other to task
and smoke, like a sluggish anaconda
recoils and glides on polished glass.
A fair day you might say, for a market,
or driving heavy beasts to the buyers
along the first rime frost of the roadside.
So much for reality: the warm smell of cattle,
thick coats, hot whiskies, and ashsticks
prodding the side-stepping bullocks.
So much for late October and the season,
a cruel five month journey into March
and the frozen fields all scorched of shelter
as the clock and the year run down.
La Grande Armée crosses the stubble land
as the teeth of a harrow rake,
black horses cross the window panes,
glacial patterns, Cossacks in the shape
of scald crows scrabble on the make.
Pinioned in winter the question becomes
year's beginning or season's end?

Falling Down Borges' Stairs

This is the step that is conjointed
with a joist somewhere in the sinking house;
despite its symmetry is out of true
a perfect image of a battle-field, anonymous
and sometime after bare of trees
that bloomed and burgeoned on the hessian coloured map
(curled edges on the camp-site table top,
the lamp asquint — light slanting from the left
corners held down by cigars and shells and lead)
& the nostalgic wind-blown wafts of paraffin
such as fill the white nights, water and cognac,
the soot that smudges on the tent,
& the Emperor, secure within his tunic, nightly
must decide with stabbing index finger
which companies he must deploy, what hooves will mark
the paper with upturned symbols of good luck —
the same that turn the race-course upside down;
the Louis d'Or that ride upon a jockey's yoke
tumbling askew between sky and earth.
The Equestrian School and the forge present
for him, for me, not much — perhaps a moment
just before the choice; one could retreat, retrench,
before experience of second thought. My
foot upon the stairs is led forever down
these blood-mottled steps; mirrored in sabre and boot

For Jack Walsh d. London 1973

No, it does not surprise me that men die
but that they live so long against all odds
and, running their fingers on the table learn
again the splinter-points of braille, the bark
of trees grown brown and bent long journeys past;
a name in lacquer on a box
across the years, across the years; all chaff.
Forgive me; I have not forgot your foreign city garden
nor gravel paths, your cypress trees,
the endless exploration of your petrolled weeds;
I know the cells, the bones, the fluid of the brain,
you, drying frayed electrode that tumbles in the ground
and in the earth seeks out the waning moon —
& old friend I'll welcome-in each deep new year
and eat the speed and flash of sap and root,
take home the wound of sunlight from the stone
and pray your present river air and reed be keen;
as mine, your best works stand unfinished . . .
spring time and autumn, a circle of bright roads

oh God deny me not the time to learn my own design —
an old man in blue evenings beyond the fear of windows —
who answers clearly through the falsity of lines
that life is, is glorious, and flawed. Not polished;
undiminished.

Derryribeen. Westport. June 16th 1975

I pray you peace, you household gods
while daylight lasts; and the globed lamp burns.
today with trowelled hands I picked
mortar from between the bricks;
dust of years on your packed earth floor;
congealed; new smoke from the sunken grate
stormed like Djinns through the wall,
fingered a lapsed corner of the thatch;
your gallery three oleographs, a pope, two saints,
and good enough for Greco's ecstasies.
this cruel-toothed trowel proceeds
along the surfaces, the crevets, the edge of stone
interstices; I come upon a hollow place —
a rooted, peasant, catacomb,
and here, I see, you hid your folded hair,
the seasoned clippings of your nails,
pathetic, nameless, but remembered etcets.
all marked collect.
I offer you no hurt & nor do I disturb, distract.
this evening, quiet as sleeping trees,
household gods; I pray your peace.

Leather Tourniquet

Those Egyptians knew their teeth
caries and cavities
and the mythological road from Rathgar
(bottles of stout and boxes of matches)
slung in their lantern jaws;
two thousand years, I ask you,
the mummied fossil answers to the X-rays
combs back its yellow hair from brow
and reaches hands across the centuries —
incipient messages from me to you;
clickety-click it's (static) six six six
and God alone knows who comes through the door
this time. Blue eyes upon a dot
upon the microfilm of the ages;
but, ever in green fields, the eyes that stare,
the needle-pointed pupils
corn-flower blue, the iris black as lunar
landscapes, as bare as southern Spain,
wandering the void of the retina edge.
And that, believe me, was a dance.
I saw a woman whinny in the Portobello Star
her lip drawn back upon her canines,
the blood upon her arm, the two sweet pearls
too sweet by half aside her mouth,
avuncular and murderous I offered her black leather
and tasted her neck in my teeth. Wry,
spittled and be-done; the brand saliva
hawser that betrays — upon a moment opening —
like tears, a viaduct, a stem upon the
orifice, from lip to lip, trailing, trailing,
sputum. Those Egyptians knew their teeth
and stood outside a locked-up Sphinx
carrying sand-bags empty of songs, at
three o'clock in the Portobello Road.

Vade Mecum

Sailing half-over the indigo sea
think of me winging past the Crofton Hotel & the Comet
and remember you're to bring me back
snake-skin jackets, barn owls and alligators,
hoots of trains for my funeral
— sometime in the future —
&, Particularly, the brake-man, you know him
quote flagging down the Double E's
and come back to Erin — to empties, the cat,
full refuse sacks and me . . .
not everyone would see you go so quietly
— dial a mug on the subway —
they joked, I see no joking in it,
time-less, in the middle of the night
I sit with an empty glass, the 'phone,
and make to write a poem:
St. Paul in Minnesota on my birthday —
have an ironic drink for Baudelaire and me,
Scott FitzGerald's gin and tonic
or Martini or Bourbon oh how Martinis nearly killed me,
or knowing me a pint of beer,
cerveza — the largest you can find:
take good care of yourself, beware the hospitality
and I'll do like for like in kind

Days of 1979. Morocco, Ten Years After

My writ no longer runs large
God knows I eat, but sit here disparate
on a Muslim Prayer-Mat, on a chair;
unleavened, yet they leave me
alone in the cold and shaky world;
for what, for silence between words,
obscenities and drunken masquerades
— the pose might leave a much paraded air —
Do you sweat when we? Lady do you sweat;
or yet the transpiration when we don't;
angels' wings at every orifice
transmogrify, give air-vents to the bar,
the sunlight hides behind the door —
a fiddler's welcome and a curse:
Nosferatu: enter of your own accord;
— and with beards and neuroses they arrive
recognisable, by times clean-shaven,
a Gallery at the gate. Lunacy obtains;
I keep it back & keep it back —
the second-hand that slithers to the left
and leftwards, always, down the stairs
and the music that must never stop;
The Topless Towers of Ilium
half-glimpsed but always from afar;
the red-dust roads, those desert paths,
Coming down the road from *Sidi Rahal*
Macour said couchez soleil: couchez soleil,
at sunset; comme il couche El Glaoui.

Jack Walsh

There will be a meeting
most short, I grant you,
on the early-morning stair-case
you died before I ris you
Gorey-wise & shaped like swans
there will be a meeting
on the stair-case
or maybe in Joan Radnor's room
should I say it
all the dead come home
and rest and take it easy
true derelicts of norms
and that would be a meeting
you silver green, and out of face,
long nails, I'd take it,
rip my breast & make me drink
you bearded why not
the grave demands grave-cloths,
but there will be a cerement,
Jack, sweetheart, I offer forms.

Sequence For Carrington

1.
Perhaps
it was initially, a question of torpedoes.
Long and slim-line; but previously washed,
greased, ampersand made good again. Water
might sometimes lick them, all over, no
rationalisation; no touch of words, no sharks
to seven-tooth the vision, all alone; I ask
for Carrington, no cures, no songs, but maybe
— a Malaguena for example — a start
and always, tipped-hat, slow and easy, in mind
of the terrible turning horn
that drives and misses but an inch of depth;
how much between the pistol & the fingers
and the clutch;
or yet the pool,
those mad, misguided, farmyard hens
that turn their sly becoming backs upon the nest

2.
Who laid the boot-print at my door step?
too large, too deep, for any yet;
& that mis-shapen creature half-strangled
after birth, who calls and leaves a master-card;
the question mark —
much mysteries within the mind. Remark
upon her scudding quarters; her scuttled walk;
& when she knocks upon your door
may you be ready; angst; and waiting — for
she is clean; she lopes along a cat-walk,
and stand you back for she has claws —
retractable, an impulse from the brain;
& Carrington, sit tight,
encircled,
it is not yet the dreadful death
that seems to lead you
to the pistol's mouth

3.
A chance glance at an autograph
a name for maybe, or the time called up,
you kept me wideawake for many nights;
tonight an anvil and a preacher
will keep me perfect from my sleep;
enough for that & I'd be pale
or tender, bring you basins full of sea-food;
oh I'd consume, consuming
the salt flesh of your eyes; the lizard stalks
& all the while outside of this resuming
the small talk in the garden,
extending cucumbers sliced in a dish;
excitement thin as acid in the rind,
your afternoons leave something tart upon the tongue

4.
You know it was not gentle in the garden —
the lilac blooms and fades;
witch-hazel turns and bites; the picture hats
do not persuade;
nor the well-stitched thatch, the afternoons
demanded much in the plane shade —
a name, perhaps, too quickly stated,
a bridle on the sight cannot prevent the single
dangerous, unguarded glance
upon the lilies and the still, green, pond
and the greener evil stillness just beyond;
that quivering, damp, unease,
that nets you, dead, among the smiling faces
that surround
your tangled, loving, afternoons —
the sculpted head that summons from the ivy
with curved stone mouth & hollow eyes
that see you clearly over all the conversation
dancing most courageously your dance
'a green fan broken by the wind'

For My Grandmother, Nora Wooloughan

If you knew how dependent I was
on nicotine, alcohol and pills
& how the fear of someone's dying
rasps on my ragged antrum
the zig-zag picture of the hills —
my rotten jawbone — action, beat, or stills,
you would not leave me in the half-light
but ask me how it kills
my understanding of the hospitals
'and those who wait
till waiting does' & fills the corridors:
people at oraisons?
an old lady with a slice cut from her ear,
so many homes she'll not re-enter
though nearer her friends and near;
one morning she will not re-open
the bits and pieces, holy cross and holy shrine,
two honed and polished razors:
— the razors underneath the bed are mine:
she said so: and blind as slugs the hawks
will find her hiding place,
a grey-trail grimace from the mouth
& in their lips of paraquat insoluble
or worse;
dear little lady, I'll curse them
with an apse — lay one single hand upon you
or your bags — that never saw to ask
& you alive and with us what your bright wishes were
. . . Such vanities, your slim ears and your hair;
the house in Seville Place where all your people were;
Helen for North Wales;
Lily Greenham for Argentina;
Larry for the desert of Australia, painting
Churches,
& the Cattle Boats to Birkenhead.

your Cameos, black Twenties Lace, Gold Chains,
the jet that rattles, pin-point in a bodice,
the musk that settles in a wardrobe;
a dress you never wore perhaps & what remains?
The fact I loved you for you held a pound maintains
its hayfeed value & your treasures . . .
— ah your treasures they were mine
to sift out in a cedar wood cigar-box, old
photographs, beyond the shuttle and the bobbin and the thread.
as time is in your 84th year
no catskins, furlough or antithesis: I
leave it simply this:
You, time-lived lady, in your long-pinned hats,
may you for ever be,
    may you arrange.

Cassandra Speaks About The Irish Famine

Give me that sharp knife, the butcher's cutlass
that shall lacerate your womb,
do not endear me when the knives are sharp
do not sleep easy in your homes;
by times the night-winds slip in easy
and occupy your beds
the dead horse and the dead rider
are threatening your gods. What distaff
would you offer in the compound! Tchah!
would it even matter — a whiff in the nostril —
I speak of blood and a universe that couldn't listen,
there is blue-stone in the mountains —
in spring rivers gold glitters
think before you make a time of rags and flitters
& hand me that sharp knife, the butcher's cutlass,
better to cut out the sore
than die, begotten, eating reeds in ditches

The Wicked Messenger

They say he used to send her
dismembered parts of animals,
as frogs' legs — flesh split from flesh —
or spawn in a galvanised bucket,
and that nightly she would take them,
owls' limbs, the backs of alligators,
& crustaceans of the breathless world
& the dinosaurs that sing in trees
& he was waiting for a watch-face
in the early early morning light
as blue as blue as ever was:
they say he sent her shell-fish
& dead men in a bottle,
a handful of dice thrown down on the carpet,
match-sticks in a fire-place,
spilt stains upon the shining tiles;
they say he sent her
torn packets and brown paper parcels;
carapaces of minotaurs,
mushrooms in a garden
feathered by the wind;
they say he used to send her
such cold gifts
and bits and pieces of his mind

Knocking Holes In Fontainebleau

Knocking holes in walls
knocking holes in walls
knocking holes in walls
for the sun to come through
and the glass is ten past zero
and the client feeds us cats
and the gaffer's in the cafe
knocking back the pastis
and he's making like a hero
because he knows this work's a bastard
and the client's cut the power off
to prevent us making phone calls
and the dust gets up your nostrils
and the French do charge for water
and we're knocking holes in mortar
and we haven't got a kango
and we haven't got a comb and
we haven't got a chisel-head
just a couple of French shovels
and some equidistant hammers
and we're knocking holes in mortar
and we're inching through the drystone
and we're taking down the levels
of this Ice Station Zebra
and Alistair MacLean now
must dig for all he's worth
not a sign of P. MacGoohan
we are too far South of North
and we won't find a Polaris
not here in Fontainebleau
we're surrounded by the forest
where Dutch dumping is illegal
and we're knocking holes in drystone

and we're raking out the mortar
and they're serving up the carnivores
with apples in their houses
drink freezes in this atmosphere
the G.I.s need hot chocolate
and we're knocking holes in drystone
and we're knocking holes in mortar
and we're knocking holes in walls
and we're knocking holes in windows
just to let the sun through
just to let some sun through

Ophelia, Sing To Me

There is a cliff beyond my bedroom window,
four floors falling turning over,
there is a door that opens inwards
& I lack a mirror & thus I never see
whose face grins over my shoulder . . .
a revenant and reject from Cervantes —
formed out of glass & so translucent —
though if he be the one I think
there is no surface that could take his print
no casting-light from any planet . . .
But I have heard the serpent hissing, waiting
in the garden, keeping vigil night by night
in the Plain of Umbria & then in Dublin,
nor can the serpent move on glass
nor could this serpent cast reflection
(I'll make a ghost of him as lets me . . .
& walk the battlements of Elsinore.
There is a cliff beyond my bedroom window
and the unappeasing dark. No Munich, Father,
God forgive us all this thankless task.)
and I watch the silver moon through glass
and yet record some aspect of this world . . .
I'll make a ghost of him as lets me —
A strawman on an open road;
he walks expectantly before me leaving shoes
and folk-lore traps and dervish leaves,
he waits in some deserted country lane
against the ditch beneath the dripping winter trees
We'll meet in Sticksville, Deathstyx County,
On the Sticksville Prohibition Train

O Bakelite Miz Moon

Jump a hundred times
and then get laid
this is no horror movie
but late at night and I'm afraid
I tried to say I couldn't sleep
a bottle to my mouth
but looking backward over time
there's no sense of drought
& I believed you when you told me
that all green cheques were green —
green-backs, slap a dollar
this lady has been seen
in Banks with her machine-gun
holding up her own
I will salute you and respect you
oh bakelite Miz. Moon.
A heart-break on the telephone
sparks off a certain lapse
a gentle lady in her cradle
an age, a meaning, and a breast;
we must have met light-years back
by the evil-winded sea
when you displayed your cuff-links
in your bed of porphyry,
did you amid the daylight
when the hours had crawled away
& they locked you in the close wing
— every Swan must have her day —
find it written on the ceiling
as a moustache curling outward
a black and nonsense notion
did you find my lips too turgid
in the sex-scenes in the Motel

where we played Bianca Jaggers
sate Doctors of Divinities
and nurses at your elbow
while we reckoned hours in ounces
and made it down the highway
& I believed you when you told me
that the road had no horizon
as you smiled beneath your vizor
as you checked your magazine
and you got us to tomorrow
my sweet bakelite Miz. Moon.

The Last Machine

Flowers that turn to faces
shame endeavours
time the hours and the measure
bilocate the morning iris
& turn again Renewed Inflections
in an eye;
flowers that turn to faces
in the weave, the loam, the leap,
crossed roads of darkness,
or the returning eyes of God
white and silent on the altar, please
no medication:
could be peace, a swift transit & after
that my disbelieving friends
the Golden Horde of Sammerkand
the mongols ride in also
loose limbed of metal —
what safe-house could so withstand
the black-haired mother & her daughter
swinging on a bandstand & shuffling
always shuffling after:
perhaps a glimpse of Heraclitan green
would set a limit on the harbour
& set a limit on their secrets
not just their item secrets but their language
my tongue to yours: mot juste:
and could you ever after taste it
as ashes and pearls in Warsaw? Hein?
Of course I'm just enquiring
for there are other ditches
and thousands yet to crowd them;
speak easy, speak into this leather (pause)
this leather microphone,
poor biforked miserable ghast
and where do you come nestling from?
A point upon an apex? Really?

Have I so put my trust in metronomes?
have I so put my trust
have I so put
have I
the sunlight shines through the window
so Heaven is maybe warm
as Syracuse and with it blue
as the Creature From The Black Lagoon
and at this point in time, Dear God,
whoever but James Dean?
Sunlight, boots, a beat up limousine;
the ever present questions
the lips carved out of rock
I ask most consciously
in all this sliding syntax
for that last bullet from the last machine.
Sweet Alphaville,
sweet adeline.
And that gaunt black-walled prairie house
demesne.

Eight Hours to Prove the Artefact

Well now Miz Moon
do you remember what you recollected
& you remaining (still American) intact?
let's put our heads together and resume
what we both know to be a lie in fact
our sad relationship:- and yet at that
not all unreal but getting fairly urgent
because at last the news is out Miz Moon
your time is up & you are coming back
and some are ready here and waiting
come in my love the window's open
& each black fish that swims the ocean
may curl upon your own moonlit neck
Friends can't you hear her? Buvons à Zelda
Miz Moon is climbing up the stairs
& life itself is turning dangerous
though Christ alone knows how we've wasted
& spent the night-times riding sleepers
for fear of being the next day's wreck
but let us get this in perspective
word is Miz Moon you're coming back
& we will have a blitzed-out evening
which will not please the Doctors but
our inner organs peeled and then some
Miz Moon you're home and welcome

The Hospital Cafeteria

greetings Mr. Diver
I suppose it's no surprise
seeing you here
The liver — he said — Collapse?
What kind of death would that be?
Well — said I — (thinking on my feet) —
What price range did you have in mind?
Something off the shelf say
Or an exclusive designer all stops out
Little Black Number?
Well no — he said laughing — Neither
Really but a poor old bugger
Took an hour and a half the other night
And I was wondering
overhead Mr. Diver
plays another nervous jink
on the high wire
The artist clapped his hands he said —
There was a noise in his throat
Kind of gruff a strange hoarse noise
He sounded like a cow
There were two in there with him
A Bible a Nurse and a Doctor
— I looked over the partition —
They couldn't do anything really Nothing
That I could see he was getting on
I suppose and that was it just looking
And I was wondering
holyroller Mr. Diver
jerks a reversible double sommersault
into his coffee cup

Shades Of Ranelagh 1984
(for Niall)

As I came in from Drowned Lake Mountain
starved of money and dry to the bone, when
many long burned out years ago I was
caught good & proper on a nail spike streetscape,
another exploded sixties myth I was
caught good & proper on a judge's ruling
and my schooldays wheeled up Ranelagh Road.
As usual indiscipline I found me walking
before and after all along Vergemount
where the Muckross girls drift by like clouds.
Is original sin still alive and well
on the shaded paths of the Dodder?
Does the fashion parade throw a daily shape
to the bridge and Portobello,
does everything stop by the Grand Canal
including the four ten bus to Yuma?
Are the celluloid cowboys up in the Sandford
still yodelling the blues in pure valerian,
taking tokes and pulling strokes
on the high chapparal of the fire escape
where Homer nods to Rowdy Yates?
As I sail in from Drowned Lake Mountain
on a nineteen forties turf-boat order
I sight my boat on the filled-in harbour
and dance my jigs without embargo,
by the Grand Canal where all things stop
my ballast is sticks of selskar rock

Houserules

Hoop-la said my working wife
this woman says there were two kinds of amazons
(and she looked at me over her tee ell ess)
the ones who went in for househusbands
and the others . . . random copulators
who only hit the ground in spots

Measuring-up to my responsibilities
I called to my wife starting out for work
could you take my head in to town today please
have my hair cut and my beard trimmed
for this poetry reading on Thursday
(I was dusting my high-heeled Spanish boots)

Gladly: she threw the talking head
in the back of the car with her lecture notes
her handbag fur coat and galley proofs
tricks of trade and mercantile accoutrements
Otrivine stuffed firmly up my nostrils
to stop catarrh and Hacks for my throat

Leaving me headless and in some straits:
considering the ways of well set-up amazons
as I fumbled helplessly around the garden
playing blind man's buff to a dancing clothesline
stubbing my pegs on air and thinking with envy
of my neighbour and his empire of cabbages

Three Figures In A Pub With Music

And since it has to be a pub scene faute de mieux
take one fat man spread upon a bar stool
talking of Billie Holliday's Strange Fruit
                                        Garrotted by the slit eyes
on his left he launches into relativity
Einstein he says was only his opinion
and don't ever — lifts glass — degenerate opinion
                                        The instruments
I admire the most are the trumpet and the voice
I don't Strange Fruit remember if the blacks were free
he lurches through an instantaneous high C

and slit eyes picks up faultless on the melody
O Mein Papa and Eddie Calvert was magnificent

                                       His dexterous friend
the donkey-jacket-over-duck-egg-blue despite
initial difficulty in the depth of field
regains some clarity of tone and brain and pitch
                                      (why am I so Black & Blue)
while slit eyes does a private quick-step to the jacks
and disappears the props and stools are switched
on absent friends the orchestra lights up the two
                                  with martial music
for chat of history and politics and work and sex
and first name heads of state and drink and revolution
and melting dusty ice fills up the cracks

                                      the dying notes
of Tipperary Far Away in Spanish Harlem

Days of May 1985
(for Niall)

In the village street a stained-glass artist
Is trawling the shops for Brunswick black
On a morning when my mind is taken up with light
And light effects on silver halides

Or in Russells on a bleary Wednesday
Clients push in chafing and shooting their cuffs
Signalling pints but 'spirits out first please'
Such are the limits of a year's horizons

This week brought Paul Durcan's postcard
With news of Robert Frost and mention of Mt. LaFayette
A catalogue of timber in New Hampshire
And yesterday my wife sailed in from Paris

To find me dressed again in campaign summer gear
Which doesn't differ much in truth from winter's
The addition or the stripping of a layer plus decorations
For my regimental Thursdays in the mad house

Being thus strappadoed I must have my story straight
And in my ley-lines find a bill of credence
Pick up on Leeson Street where I was born —
In the Appian Way my bones of childhood mock me

Yet these May mornings toiling to the Nursery
I sense my father's ghost in the wheeling migrant birds
And soon I can accept the electric invitation
Of my amazing son to the breathless world of cherry flowers.

Closeup

He is my neighbour yet
he puzzles me — he is a threat up there
guarding the summer shoulder of the hill
perched upon sticks and busy as an insect
                                          first time we met
he choked off my tentative *buon giorno*
(and ever since although his wife replies)
                                                  gruff and locked
in the narrow gauge of his daily
crab-slide from his doorway to the shade
and the waiting car seat set
by the furnace wall beneath the autumn grapes

he is a *bella figura* man of substance

                                                his photograph
will find due place
with the others ranked along the cemetery wall
the Bevagnas and the Rossis not in prayer

but as now in slippers and woollen cap he stares
down the ridges of the valley to the road below
a partisan planning an ambush

or putting order on the seasons
he has marshalled them and marked them out with feast days
crippled he is impervious to accident
                                          or weather
it is September now and he is out to check
that polythene is fastened on the wood piles
stirrup pump in hand he stumps the barricades
he is opaque and undefeated
                                      and why
should I know more about him than this bare account
reckoned against such camouflage
the wind picks up and whispers through the graveyard

that is all
soon they will be tying down their houses for the winter
the year is done

green lizards dart fearless in the noonday vines
where light itself is sharp and green

Agello September 1985

Lazarus In Fade Street, Summer 1986

This afternoon in Fade Street in the sun
all these ancient gestures
and all those flickering acid lights
they . . . *don't touch me any more*
come home from harvesting the years
I have gathered in my tribe and wives
and tied the haggard door

thinks Lazarus in Fade Street in surprise

come home at last to roost
like a retired sea captain
without support or sycophants
I am watching how the operators work
taking a bearing in my own backyard
on the shifting of brick and emphasis
the architecture of the New Ireland
and noticing the architects by name

Oh Alice Glenn
Lady of Astronomical Compassion
Pray for us now and in Leinster House Amen

and I feel I was more cherished underground:

consistent in my generation
spent maybe twenty years entombed
just looking out and listening to the rain
achieving wisdom and no position
a nineteen sixties solipsist
filling in the cracks in time until
the door swung open and I shook myself awake
rolled off my bed of snakes
and travelled home like a fault to roost
a cherished child of the State

my pockets full of unsigned cheques
faded unpresented dreams
manifests of phantom ships
dry salt I gathered off Cape Horn
dry salt for wounds the curing of:

no need for gothic narrative thinks Lazarus

Ronald Reagan is made a Doctor of Laws
pray for us now and in Leinster House

something is happening here

Peter Barry is selective in his strictures
I listened hard but heard
no echoes of outrage when Tripoli was bombed

*and I don't know what it is
do you Mr. Bones?*

And yes . . . who speaks for me in this
coming up out of the ground
a fading Signorelli figure strayed from Orvieto
making my way home from Waldo's Wood?
I feel threatened in this referendum
by the aggressive razz-ma-tazz of Family Men
I have a family but I cannot share
the appalling certainty of Padraig Flynn:

who conjures me in Fade Street?

Lazarus without an audience
emerging into daylight stumbles in the dust
steadies himself by the Castle Market
consults his chart and makes for home
the high road home from Cesena

veteran of hospital and lock-up
here's where we part company perhaps
finding another way through the waste lots
turning off at the fireworks factory

and singing: *flat road yellow moon*
coming home at night through fields of sunflowers

Agello/Dublin. Summer 1986

Stopping The Lights, Ranelagh 1986
(for Niall)

1.
Two hands to the bottle of Wincarnis
this timeless gent his cap turned back to front
arranges himself in the delta of downtown Ranelagh
and sits on the public bench first
carefully hitching his trousers at the knee
preserving the delicate break over the instep
advised by Bertie Wooster's Jeeves
he hefts the bottle up and sucking deep
with one eye shut he draws a bead

Secure in his well constructed tree top hide
Lord Graystokes fixes on the jungle
in between the changing of the traffic lights
like drops of blood the amber jewels of his rood
accurately lights a cigarette
The lion — he mouths — *The lion sleeps tonight*
the traffic beacons change
controlled and manageable their peacock march
from green to red and red to green
Ring out wild bells: he settles back

A businesslike nun swims into frame
intervenes in a pale cold car behold
and disengaging gear
reflects a while in Gordon's hardware shop
the glass of her aquarium is hung
with buses plastic basins toasters
electric kettles lengths of timber super-glue
bronze fire-dogs brooms and Bilton dinner-sets
here on the veldt
she brings a missionary whisper
the folded mysteries of convent breakfasts
white linen and starched altar cloths
white cattle birds half glimpsed in Africa
lights flash cars slip into gear slide off

And the delta has become my launching pad
my swampland Florida
junkyard of burnt out rocket systems
where all that thrust falls back to earth
to rust in secret in the Corporation Park
my blue eyed son is friend to man
and guides me through the shadowy tangled paths
where alligators twine and lurk
and I learn to recognise my lunar neighbours
among mysterious constellations

   2.
It takes some time to make an epic
or to see it for the epic that it is
an eighteenth century balloonist
when Mars was in the Sun set out for Wales from here
trailing sparks ascended through the clouds
and sank to earth near Howth
while dancing masters in the Pleasure Gardens
played musical glasses in the undergrowth
they have used the story to rename a pub
to make a Richard Crosbie of the Chariot and

We too have come through dangers and we call
to the MC on the console *stop the lights*
here at the wrong end of the telescope
my one concern is holding down the present
Sunday mornings on the Great South Wall are real
and hand in hand with Niall it is enough
when we are astral travellers and our astral turf
the cut blocks that interlock upon each other
and we are inaccessible and far off dots
on the Half Moon road to the lighthouse
safe from the law alive and well
in the wind on the Great South Wall

Annaghmakerrig 1986